Seeds of Gravity

An Anthology of Contemporary Surrealist Poetry from Ireland

Edited by Anatoly Kudryavitsky

SV

SurVision Books

First published in 2020 by
SurVision Books
Dublin, Ireland
www.survisionmagazine.com

Introduction © Anatoly Kudryavitsky, 2020
The poems © their individual authors, 2020
This collection copyright © SurVision Books, 2020
Design © SurVision Books, 2020

ISBN: 978-1-912963-18-8

Acknowledgements

Grateful acknowledgement is made to the editors of the following, in which a number of these poems originally appeared:

The American Journal of Poetry; Banshee; Big River Review; Boyne Berries; The Brain of Forgetting; Cyphers; Diaphanous; A Glimpse Of; The North; Gog and Magog by Ciaran O'Driscoll (Salmon Poetry, 1987); *Life Monitor* by Ciaran O'Driscoll (Three Spires Press, 2009); *A New Ulster; Numéro Cinq; Otoliths; Poethead; Poetry Salzburg Review; The Quarryman; Rochford Street Review; The Seventh Quarry; Southword; Star*Line; Street Line Critics,* Helsinki, September 2015, curated by Lotte Bender; *Surrealists and Outsiders—2018 anthology* (Thrice Publishing, Roselle, Illinois, 2018); *Surrealists and Outsiders—2019 anthology* (Thrice Publishing, Roselle, Illinois, 2019); *SurVision; Ten Years in the Doghouse* (Doghouse Books 2013, ed. by Noel King); *Visions International.*

CONTENTS

Introduction

In the first half of the twentieth century, no Irish poets were out and out surrealists. Samuel Beckett and his circle, Thomas MacGreevy, Brian Coffey, George Reavey, and Denis Devlin can be described as modernists with strong surrealist tendencies. Still, these poets planted the seeds of Surrealism in Irish literature. "Although Irish poets have not until now been identified as such, it is not surprising that they are magic realists and surrealists, given the resource of our rich heritage of myth, legend and folklore," the Limerick-based poet Ciaran O'Driscoll once stated.

Literary Surrealism really came to Ireland in the second half of the twentieth century. David Gascoyne's own work, as well as his translations from the French surrealists, opened the new horizons for some Irish poets. Many others were influenced by grotesque and often apocalyptic overtones in Dylan Thomas's poetry. Among those who followed this trend were such poets as Ciaran O'Driscoll and Medbh McGuckian. O'Driscoll, whose work has been popular among the Irish readers of poetry ever since the 1980s, is the link between the two surrealist groupings of Irish poets. He admired Brian Coffey and Denis Devlin, and he took up where they left off, eventually developing his own, unique style. According to the critic Michael S. Begnal, reviewing O'Driscoll's *The Speaking Trees*, "his poems often conjure dream-like or visionary states... His language is clear and deliberate but describes a bizarre or surreal subject matter."

The next generation of writers gave us such surrealist-minded poets as John W. Sexton, Afric McGlinchey, Matthew Geden, Tony Bailie, and Tim Murphy. They all are inclined to search for their versions of Surrealism in a more textual, intuitive area of thinking. Their poetics are complex; they, to quote the well-known essay by the American surrealist poet Charles Borkhuis, write "from inside language." According to Borkhuis, there's a distinction between the "orthodox" Surrealism of Breton and the work of "later or tangential writers, influenced by Surrealism but antithetical to its orthodoxy." If orthodox Surrealism is about "transition from image to image," as Charles Bernstein once put it, tangential Surrealism is more about transmutation, or leaps, from word to word, from phrase to phrase.

Colin O'Sullivan, writing in *Dublin Review of Books,* describes Kerry-based John W. Sexton as "one of Ireland's major, and criminally underrated poets." His experiments took him on many a wondrous poetic journey; he explores the surreal in nature, be it wildlife or the human mind's reflection on it. Afric McGlinchey, a writer from West Cork, once described her poetic devices by stating that she "makes associations between individual and landscape, between our minds and our physical bodies; our cultural and familial histories; our longings and our losses." Surrealist approach and commitment to the integrity of her "materials" have become essential to her method. Tim Murphy, originally from Cork but living in Spain, draws on the French Surrealist tradition to present haunting imagery that challenges the reader's poetic horizons, and his work also tends to explore a textual, sentient zone. Scottish poet, Helena Nelson, has likened his poetry to "a series of paintings that draws in all kinds of symbols".

Reviewing poetic works by Tony Bailie, a poet and novelist from Belfast, Richard Montgomery wrote about his "stripped to the waist style of poetry." Following in the footsteps of Artaud and Beckett, minimalist poets like Tony Bailie and the Cork poet Matthew Geden outlaw most literary devices or even emotional colouring; they focus their attention on individual words or phrases, sometimes rearranging them on the page so that their most basic and individual properties disclose something unexpected about themselves, something unmistakably surreal.

This collection of poems offers different approaches to poetry writing, and let us hope that the readers will open up to the new poetics. Tangential Surrealism, already widespread in English-speaking countries, seems to have found its way to Ireland and, hopefully, is here to stay.

Anatoly Kudryavitsky, Dublin, April 2020

TONY BAILIE

Tony Bailie works as a journalist, travel writer and environmental columnist for *The Irish News* in Belfast. He has had two previous collections, *Coill* and *The Tranquillity of Stone*, both published by Lapwing Publications. Two novels, *The Lost Chord* and *ecopunks*, were published by Lagan Press. His novella *A Verse to Murder* is available as an ebook. His chapbook titled *Mountain under Heaven* won James Tate Poetry Prize in 2019, and was published by SurVision Books later that year.

Premonition

Time lurks, a shadow
in a half-opened doorway
waiting to swoop and engulf
the raw, unrefined night,
when all is still potential,
the shape of events unmoulded,
mere suggestions
of memories to come.

Helix

City streets loop and spiral
a DNA helix
curling and weaving in and out of itself
identity fractured
the essential I-ness gathered up and hurled
into the fractal swirl
a mesh of directions
that tangle and merge
and drift into flaying strands of snake-hair
a bag woman on a rain-drenched hill
I pass
avoiding stone-turning eyes
faint odour of sweat and stale piss
the hiss of wind whipping her hair
slurp of chapped lips
on the butt of a fag
fallen Medusa in winter.

Ash

Bruised knuckles bulge
on brittle branches,
festering knots
tensed and waiting
for their locks to be sprung,
to spew their store
of infant leaves,
sprawl and suckle
on April rain,
then stretch out in the sun
and shuffle in a breeze,
cast shifting shadows
that gather and devour
those who lurk beneath them.

Binary Affair

Her pupils are tiny pinpricks of black,
twin dark stars
from another universe
drawn into parallel orbit
around our sun,
impenetrable specks of diamond
from which no light escapes,
compact and dense,
their gravity pulling me in
to a place where time has warped
and space is squeezed,
where the din of city traffic
has been compressed into a solar wind
that carries me
on an interstellar roar,
flaying and helpless
I am flung through her inner space,
hurled out sobbing and bleeding.

Destination

Tendrils of weed
haul the rusted axle
down to earth,
encasement of clay,
the memory of daytrips
and blurred open roads
fractured and flaking,
clumps of nettle
and dandelion clusters
smother once glinting steel,
machine-wrought precision
mangled and blistered,
journey's end
in an overgrown field.

Star Aleph 151169

A draft from a dungeon
carries a lone voice,
whispered pleas for freedom
that mix and swirl
with a cloud of dust
captured in a shaft of light,
a universe summonsed
by the swish of a rat's tail.
Four inches from the floor
above a moulding sack
lies a galaxy
with 10 billion stars
in the shape of the symbol Om
and in a segment of space
called the Ox's Horn,
by those who can observe it,
orbiting a blazing sun
lies a mountainous world
with rivers and forests
and huge churning seas
where winged creatures
flit among the trees
and sharp-toothed beasts hunt
foragers that
nestle among fallen leaves.
Sitting in a musky wood
just below a mountain pass
in a hidden, shallow cave
where candles burn

and bells chime,
a cowled figure in a half trance
listens to the forest's groan,
the creaking bark,
a dusty cough,
a prisoner moaning in his cell.

Night Sizzles

Sodium glow swirling,
yellow-tinted spiral of light
that twists and slithers
like urine down a drain,
gurgles into darkness.
Night sizzles, undulating,
electric shimmer,
tangible like static.
My hair stands on end
and I'm nervy in this sullen heat
as if possessed
and about to leap
into the rays of a black sun.

Managua

Throat-clogging dust swirls
in coned eddies,
mini-tornadoes that rise
and twirl in spiralled hoops
that suddenly collapse
and scatter chaos.
Acrid smoke
seers my eyes,
snakes in wisps,
drifting tendrils
wrap themselves around me,
lassoes cast
by spectral captors
who rise from the haze
of embers and smoke
to hover by a bonfire.

Hungry Ghost

Her powdered skin
left a musky streak
across my crumpled sheet
that I didn't clean for a week,
the faint whiff of her
lingering when I bent to sniff
before going to sleep,
the memory of our disastrous rut –
separate rhythms
that never merged
into a unified flow –
a hungry ghost hovering,
burnt-out memories
carried on a waft of ash,
that settled on my bed.

MATTHEW GEDEN

Matthew Geden was born and brought up in the English midlands. In 1990, he moved to Kinsale in County Cork, where he now works as the Director of Kinsale Writing School. In 2020, he was appointed Writer in Residence for Cork County Library and Arts Service. His collections of poetry include "Swimming to Albania" (Bradshaw Books, 2009) and "A Place Inside" (Dedalus Press, 2012), as well as "Autumn" (Lapwing, 2003), which includes his translations from Guillaume Apollinaire. In November 2019 he was Writer in Residence at Nanjing Literature Centre, China. His chapbook titled *Fruit* was published by SurVision Books in 2020.

Favourite Nymphs

The word *favourite* is to be interpreted
variously. I include some shrimps
and beetles. I doubt if the trout
cares. The old flies have many years
of life left in them yet. Torp's Reed
Smut Nymph, Shrimper, Eric's Beetle,
The Chomper, Gold Ribbed Hare's Ear,
The Grey Nymph, the Persuader, the Hatching
Midge Pupa, Pheasant Tail and No-Name.

The Storm

storm scientists make rain
a twist of test tubes
small clouds bump and grind
the crumbling laboratory walls

a whirl of lifetimes spin
past your eyes banknotes
flutter out of reach
tomorrow you will start over

rain and wind permitting

A Yellow Spot

The magic, a patch of sunlight
stains a wooden desk and a ghost
futility makes each line count,
nurses a way through the night.

The lion's mane spreads tentacles
pulls in her prey, slow pulse
crosses currents, a temporary
pain, dark waters at the shore.

Flamenco

I step out of my birthday
and into confetti; a snowstorm
mutely shakes down the skies,
a furious snowglobe roused
by the Happy Dragon, the chill
of minus seven and footprints
disappear down blind *hutong*.
I grope through swirling
streets, return with *píjiŭ*,
peanuts and frozen eyelashes.
Stepping back from the cold
I open the door into Andalucia.
It is twenty eight degrees and Enrique
Morente is teaching me Flamenco,
a gift, you say, to walk two worlds at once.

The Back of a Lorry

Fallen off the back of a lorry
nothing but the sky; an airy
emptiness that hovers above
the man-made metal, weathered
wood unsentimentally stripped
away by the years, the long
suffering blood sweat and tears
silenced by the churchyard,
a tomb marks the spot,
a stretched out wooden bed.

Refuge

What remains of summer is locked
away at night, after opening time
sun-seekers file respectfully into
a black box where a disembodied
voice in the car directs the sails
splashed in light. The beach lies
burning in the distance,
last year's tide has arrived,
rivers return to my socks,
shoes, the land, rain ravages
my throat and I seek refuge
in the conservatory of a distant country.
Years later we file out into the dark,
visas stamped in the headlights of cars.

Sonnet I

even just to enter the surf
wrapped up in funereal black
bare blubber in the bubbles
the shock of that fierce slap
tossed around and shaped
stripped to a pale bone
thrown up on the high tide
trodden down in sand

and in silence in a car
a couple watch the waves
crash down without them
almost time to go now
the sky darkens into October
and the wind roars in their ears

Sonnet II

the art of measurement
occurs in the everyday
submission to pain
in variable light
and occasional dark
ignorant of time
one more step ahead

it's not so bad really
there is a dryness
in the throat
the muscles strain
a furious dialogue
wonders how the agony
will end the pain will die

Sonnet III

there are leaves
falling from the sky
crumpled messages
fill the many pockets
loose change gathers
a careless offering

and the metro station
fills with the air of a violin
classical elegance a concert
plays out to an unembarrassed hush
the audience flows on
ineffably towards the sea

and when the music is silent
what, after all, remains?

From *Fruit*

the mirror takes you
through the undergrowth

tangled groves gone
wild with pithy beauty

a distant song might
call your first name

the one given to you
by the lonely earth

here in my hands
a ball of fire burns

ANATOLY KUDRYAVITSKY

Anatoly Kudryavitsky is from South Co. Dublin. His chapbook titled *Stowaway* was published by SurVision Books in 2018. His latest (fifth) collection, *Two-Headed Man and the Paper Life,* has been brought out by MadHat Press (USA) in 2019, further translated into Romanian and published by Editura Revers. His novel, *The Flying Dutchman,* has been published by Glagoslav Publications (UK) in 2018.

Hans Bellmer's Dolls

We all come from a doll. Also inside,
puppets, puppies and Easter eggs.
How many spare parts have been thrown in?
Three pelvises, a couple of recycled heads?
The sky is dotted with vestiges of obsession:
the dematerialisation of being, the life-size
presence of the inhuman, a hair veil
over the geometry of perturbance.
Aggressive fingers pleat the pink;
a disembodied eye is the navel.
Let's play doctor in the attic (in the Arctic),
let's invent new desires!
Of course, we'll later curse the course
of non-events.
How much longer will the unpossessible
possess us?
On the beach, our stray libido wakes up
and shakes off its fleas.

Reacaire

Somewhere in the corner of language...
—Julie Flanders

The scent of unread fields... Eternity
is hard of hearing.
Trash barges of an ideology
earth up our ears.

Our allegiances survive as hearts.
Brown ice of cedars. Triangulation.
What's the lo-call number
for the nearest time stretch?

We live the daily funeral,
the panic of atoms. Language
has many corners
sprinkled with birds' early light.

Your snow perfume, the dead warmth
of your body... A sick man
with his sack of stories
under the round book of the moon.

Reacaire: reciter of poems (Irish Gaelic)

Leeway

Now that you're swimming the light, tell us
what you ink.
Are you fired up by the radiant mouth
of yesterday's ashes? By the handheld thunder
amid ejected objects?
Oh, how we like your ubiquitous unpredictability!

In the court of awe, a gem losing its case.
The burnt umber of the day.
Magnets operate compasses.
"Don't mind my *stultitia*," says the purpose.
"Don't mind course edits," say the eddies.
Long time, no ask.

Now our "else" wants to be something else. Perhaps,
a thermal mystery. Or strawberry stars.
There's more confusion underwater
than above the clouds, more history
in the mirrors than in the eyes.
Deviate, reflect.

Stowaway

Lost in the planet wood, he imbibes solar ire
as he crosses the great divide.
A thought? An embryo?

He is dressed in caressing waves. The wind
is all salt, the infinity left ajar.
A silken lighthouse transmits his pulse
to the cloud womb.

Senselessness requires space. His face
is a non-face. He knows the way:
head first, then sideways.
He is the sum of his fears; the universe
the sum of its rubbish.
Capacity is an asset.

The slimy hemispheres are a ball of wait.
The museum of chance flowers with wily smiles,
one by one the portraits saying,
We had so many children
that some survived.

A Collage Has a Thousand Mouths

Yes, we knew that cats have a dozen eyes, but we
     never heard about matchstick horseracing.
We knew that politicians are cathedrals, but we've
     only just learned that mouths prefer solitary walks.
Go talk to the scissorman,
     to sperm flamingos.
Flap your headwings; tell this caterpillar dog
     all about leg space.
Hide your target face
     among spiderflowers.

Shadow, thy name is symmetry.
Gravity is overstretched.
You may think
a collage is an octogenarian,
but, in fact, it's an octopus.
It hides its ink.

Eva / *Ewig*

Winged plums, tearful potatoes;
the de-adornment of a portrait...
Your drum is a dream; your bell
winds the woods,
villages of darkness.

You come in, sit down.
A shaky evening, a flaked mistake.
Our branches, yours and mine;
thoughts of the same tree.
Who's crying so micaceously?

I exit. I come back in.
The bell that winds the village,
the woods of darkness.
Talking flowers, I am tired of you.
Cats and kitchens scare me immensely.

The vitality of Evita
between the sound and frozen holiness.
Loving is living your life backwards.
You bathe your indifference
in the blue pool of white.

Once in a Brazen Moon

Shadow of an arrogant ship...
How can I hear them speak? Not the dead
but the raucous pines.

Medusa would have been amused
by our hairy seaweeds. There would have been
many more hot air balloons
if it hadn't been for this war.
What's left in celestial clefts?

Collective mind is a giant grouper
that follows near-bottom flows;
individual mind, a suckerfish.
The draught of confusion, the warmth
of embarrassment. Give us all
or give us none. Who is writing history
in spent ink?

I'd do it for the light in which a loss blossoms.
I'd do it for ew.
Only the rusted are trusted, why?
I pluck at loose dulse. The flooded bed,
the torn casing of time.
Then we all fall
through a rainbow of layers.

Neutral?

We fill our great big barn with little
sesame barns where we have emptiness
sorted and stored.

Barn guards burn candles of absurd
as their lips sip smog nectar.
They sin. They sing, *Eternity will suck you in, son,*
chew you up and then unsuck you.
We won't let anybody
empty our emptiness into theirs.

The earth's hair is parting the air.
We are a natal down, disempired islanders,
and we no longer cover our nakedness
with castles and coats of armour.
Green wigs on the green.
Keep safe and wear your horseshoes
and a farmhouse harness!

So are we finally half safe?
Are these pewter soldiers
neutral or neuter?
Surrounded by money, we surrender.
The survivors like to play a little flame game
with the blame brought in on the shoulders
of gap-fillers.

Distant fires, how they cool the skin.
World history, how it hisses.

Lockdown

A tapestry of your fingerprints on the dreampane...
Existence stems from its end.
It teas like coffee, a limited edition
of a wave-crimp, a patented crib taunt.
This sternum of yours, a roadblock
against obloquy.

Today I wear quarantine grey.
The sun whistles a star-college song,
somebody gets stapled to his CV.
This smily hotel, its gaping wi-fi hotspots.
Bring me the mothball necklace
of credulous warnings.

Crystals of vision promenade with masks on.
A cemetery tune: *the earth is at its roundest
under the cross.* Children's Crusade ends
under the sands.
Would you prefer a wall of music
or the music of the walls?

Procrustes

and other dead villains play musical chairs
with historians and wild beasts.
A screech that is also a roar.
The absence of "where."
What is this place?

Outside of space, beds and memories
are scarce. Iron has been converted
into ivory. No more adventures
in synopsising & minification.

These days are best for measuring
shadows. It vexes him that their scope
extends outside a person's lifespan.
Where have all the limbs gone?

Eyeballs of the sky grow sapless.
Wasn't his "enough" enough?
Guided by puffs of manly silence,
he aspires to unwrap his inner lamb
and considers a return
to the homeland of mirrors.

AFRIC McGLINCHEY

Afric McGlinchey lives in West Cork, where she works as a freelance book editor, reviewer, and workshop facilitator. Previous collections include *The Lucky Star of Hidden Things* and *Ghost of the Fisher Cat* (Salmon Poetry), both further translated into Italian and published by L'Arcolaio. Her chapbook titled *Invisible Insane* was brought out by SurVision Books in 2019. She received an Arts Council of Ireland bursary, and was the winner of the Hennessy Emerging Poetry Award (2011).

The Green Taste of Youth

is a summer carousel, horses playing
arson, burning stables

without restraint or hold-alls
for the new world.

In the tower, light is bared
and swinging, laughing manically.

Unlatch your tongue, paint
it with saliva, spill any random

words, and spin, poi split-
time butterflies.

On the Quay of Flames

The small heir blithely bypassed the world,
staked his post to the republic of dreams,
screwing together the boards of the first living library.

On the side, two tongues, not an overcoat stranger,
something more fluid: water poured into a vase.
A footing of sinuous little replicas, twisted

into place at 5 o'clock. On the quay of flames,
the limping man drew tiny, counter Xs.
At the turn of the untilled field, his discovery:

a pure tapestry, transposition of estrangement,
resting on adopted terrain.
In rejection, there is luck.

See what happens. Leave the second stone,
turn up curios: the cosmic breath
of a soul, taking sideways form.

Preternatural alterities lurk within
furniture, gloomy canopies. They step not twice,
but endlessly into a wavy river, mingle as one.

Nostalgia is restorative. In any case,
experience the effect.
Plainly see the first day of the world.

While the Sleepers

The muse in the field
is a pop-up book.
His bed is a tongue
of grass. I am who.

I will press my finger into
the bowl of the muse's body,
place some of his dusty fire
over my eyelids.

Instead of idling
in pyjamas, I'll go
door-to-door with the dawn,
one sunrise at a time.

The Sea's Dream

The sea's dream is the ship
moving with the sun
along the indigo-edge of a child's stick horizon.

The sea's dream is the ship
fleeing an hourglass,
watched by the albatross overhead, silently.

The ship traces an ocean planet,
over the ballet of manta ray and slow-falling fish,
underwater flights from equator to pole.

The ship bends into a street of moonlight,
invites travellers to kiss
the sea's shrinking reflection

unfold vestigial gills and fly
down, down, down to the sea's secret garden,
our older memory.

A Travelling Country of Windows

All the bony roads,
spokes shaking off a mouthful
of sleet, and you
further forward than me, or inward perhaps
– a heaped bush – stop.
I know what is in that box
stiffly packaged in white canvas
– the first of the seven sorrows –
then the next to come tumbling
will be – no, let's
travel back, round the coastline up north
where the mattress groaned under
our bouncing feet and feathers flew
from the bolsters, until the creak
of a door, pink glow of the landing wallpaper.
And fast as the smallest
laughing fury, we're under the sheets:
one on the floor, pretend-sleeping,
a silence lunging from above.
Imagine it's tipping its point
like a Damocles sword.
Fleeting shock;
and then the rattling again,
struggling past the cages.

Invisible Insane

It was always the other way round.
—Margaret Atwood

Not up against a wall,
your three-legged
mind

jaywalking across
my shadow, or the city's
muddled roundabouts.

Not merging our reflections
in a winter window,
laughing at the idea

of our planet
being a snow globe
for the angels.

No matter
where, there's
no getting you

out of my mind.
Are you google
earthing me?

Is that you
I can hear, between
bells, faintly?

After the Blossoming, Boom

For Sara Baume

The raised voices of summer
petals engage, like birds,
in public relations,
contiguous with the glare
and nerves of the sun,
the scraping of chairs
and the gaping of mouths.
Alice sees through the gaps,
of course, and substitutions:
pig for fig or bird for human,
while Baume reads post-
humous feathers and snouts, still
at their barre-work, even
after the race is done.

Particle of Light through a Raindrop

If houses are lifted up and dropped, like crystal,
then shards cutting through memory.

If the cat swims, ears and nose above water,
then arms reaching to rescue.

If you hold my hand, though I feel it empty,
then rain, landing on earth and soaking it anyway.

If sun bursts from the sky, un-bedding the fog,
then, without coat, without hat, armour for a new journey.

Into the Iron Winter

sky just a body
dreaming of poppies,
silver fish

trees stare across water
towards laughter,
soft as blue moss

a mother's thin, white cup
notes her hands
around its small planet

memory
opens
its long window

hidden stars,
wind in the door,
tail in the alley

between shadows and dirt,
a girl lifts an apple
feels a bird turn

Anomie

The old philosopher, sharp as ice.
Our thinking (not upright as trees,
as we thought) is fractured by his voice.

His words conflate human agency
with the natural order,
the body of shared memory

with the vanished sign.
There should be flowers, he tells us,
in a clear-cut voice, simple as ink.

Every night, his teachings
turn to the blue laws,
or stallions, or the Book of Hours.

He invites invocation or,
at least, resistance,
to those overpouring thoughts

that have taken us down
an avenue lined
with little lamps of snow.

Tim Murphy is from Cork. He is the author of two poetry chapbooks, *Art Is the Answer* (Yavanika Press, 2019) and *The Cacti Do Not Move* (SurVision Books, 2019). His other books are *Rethinking the War on Drugs in Ireland* (Cork University Press, 1996) and *Law and Justice in Community* (with Garrett Barden; Oxford University Press, 2010). He lives in Madrid, Spain.

Route

Warred are we,
Between aqueducts we transport fire,
Between walls we design light.
We are attacked by something putrid,
Something bourgeois,
Something always wanting more.
Inert, we commission icons,
We assassinate at will;
Ever homeward bound,
Our writing is automatic.
Seven goats for the grey house ballet,
Eight horses for the deconstruction work,
A few pennies for burning our cars and shutting up—
There is a route
Out of here.

The Water Fire

See the water fire,
Blue white yellow orange red,
It creates itself from nothing:
Alive it burn-flows and alive it flow-burns.

With dry wet wave-flames
And wet dry flame-waves
The water fire preserves itself:
It is a continuous affair.

The water fire is a part of time,
Part of desire passing through time
And of time passing through desire:
It is eternal.

The water fire quenches itself,
It is immune from any dearth of reality:
Creating, preserving, destroying,
Never and always at once.

The Tipping Point

Take the days of supertramping in the lagered rain,
Of weighing each other's gold in blood, or take
The oak tree we understood, the hallucination
We made it become. Remember the portable
Passages of time, the prairie peninsulas
And the pagan ports, or when Hilma af Klint
Came to us in dreams, as the fruit of a long experience,
Showing us circles from the future...
    We are indeed all godlike,
But memory can become a satellite of betrayal,
And even if the treasure is always closer than we think,
And always waiting to be found, inhabited spirits
Cannot know this. Only the tipping point is known:
Hangmen rarely lie, and they do not avoid symmetry.

The Aurochs

For Tinna Ingvarsdóttir

Every week at a certain hour
On a certain day
I float in a sea of floating women.

The sea is clear—
In the shallow parts
You can see
Right through the water—
And every week at the same hour
On the same day,
As I float in this clear sea,
I paint universal circles,
Universal doorways:
I paint mandalas.

All the women are painting, too,
Painting as they float in the clear sea.
They paint maps with shorelines,
They paint territories with vegetation,
They paint tigers, angels and graves:
They paint the windows of their pain.

Every week at the same hour
On the same day,
When we float and paint in the clear sea,
These women and I,
We are all copying the pictures

Of the wild cattle on old cave walls;
We are all painting the bison, the wild bulls,
We are all painting the aurochs.

We paint for luck in the hunt,
We paint to cope with our trauma,
We paint our ritual need.

We paint windows of pain and we paint mandalas—
We paint the aurochs.

Mosaic

Spring body freefall dance, an elevator mosaic
In Naples, somewhere near the train station;
It is August, the day of another circus parade,
No parties, no prayers, only needles in the sun;
No words of hope or love, only boundaries
Bumping into each other, lines of control moving
Around corners of the earth, sleeping animals
Looking for any kind of comfort they can find –
The mind moves forward, it builds new mountains,
But like everything under the sun, it is divided;
Let it slip inside shadows, inside renovations,
Take the speedway and press fast-forward:
Search the stone, search the linen canvas,
Find the spring body freefall dance.

Instrumental

Sunday again.
A sombre sculpture moves
Through a highway underpass.
An empty studio is fractured
By a pious sunbeam.
A transit landscape shifts itself
To reveal a new absence,
A new marginalization.
The city prints
Another symbolic engine.
Sunday again!

Viscosity

The oils await a gilded guideline,
A canvas mark to believe in;
I wonder what is required
For things to continue like this.

The figure inspires like muslin
Primed with chalk;
The petal eyes, the stem neck,
The absence of age.

Nature is singing again,
There are divine horses on the run;
It is timely, this space deficit,
This nostalgia in an infinite loop.

There is talk on the ragwort ridge,
Gossip about the round flower-heads;
But it is merely a dawn defect,
Gauze from the other side.

Calm is restored
With new frames, with pinked skin;
It seems nothing is required
For things to continue like this.

Birds of Prey

Night's hard shoulder. Dazed, we act out,
Into a composition of parody and pain.
Notice what we've compressed.
Anger at the recurrence,
The detour of a concept.

We are in a portrait of the present,
Made warm by humanity
And dispersed like a sieve of light.

Humming along nicely, we each become
A bird of prey, you a black eagle,
I a western osprey.

Withdrawn thus by waking reality
City streets conduct us like copper wire,
Yet we block ourselves at every turn.
What's with that?

A shadow-check in the sun,
A spoken word in the thicket,
Before we know what's happening,
We each emerge with our own gold.
The old dispensation is rejected.

Heal

This ink runs its course,
As do wind and stone—
Mark the cave,
Scratch the wall.

Fight for your lifeline,
For your hopeful fear;
Fight for it, win it,
Be with it, run with it.

This energy finds light,
As do sound and space—
Paint the blue sky,
Draw the silent island.

Breach the surface,
The template of harmony;
Heal your heart,
Wake your sleeping dream.

CIARAN O'DRISCOLL

Ciaran O'Driscoll lives in Limerick. He has published eight collections of poetry, including *Gog and Magog (1987),* Moving *On, Still There: New and Selected Poems* (2001), *Surreal Man* (2006), and *Life Monitor* (2009). Liverpool University Press published his childhood memoir, *A Runner Among Falling Leaves* (2001). His novel, *A Year's Midnight*, was published by Pighog Press (2012). His chapbook titled *The Speaking Trees* was published by SurVision Books in 2018.

A Single Sound

Sometimes I wake from an afternoon nap
to a single meaningless recurrent sound –
water trickling from drains, or in a storm,
foghorn boomings from the boiler's flue.
Even when I don't know what it is,
and usually I don't, it is enough
listening to this reminder that *I am*,
outrider of returning consciousness,
herald of all things. *Why is there something
rather than nothing?* A flapping cloth,
a loose tile rattling? Better to know,
not what this certain actuality is,
but that it is, and combats entropy,
the great indifference waxing my ears.

The Lost Jockey

I suppose I always knew, deep down,
that some day it would come to this,
and I would return to the question
posed by that fellow Magritte;
to Chlotho, Lachesis and Atropos,
and snake-haired goddesses,
the Furies or the Fates
or whoever it is they are
who are in hot pursuit.
And when such an event occurs,
erupting on the ordinary scene,
there's always someone watching
from behind a crimson curtain,
who has seen it and says nothing,
only to suffer, thirty years on,
a kind of falling apart.
In the Lowlands they call it the KZ Syndrome
when the truth sprouts from the brain's spindles,
ridiculous but no longer containable.
Was it that he caught my eye
as he galloped past in flight
from those Invisibles,
his face that of an ill-starred child
hidden in the attic for fear of visitors?
There has been far too much geometry
in these parts, the regime
has been far too regular,
and begged a madness to break out,
a thundering of hooves along the drives.

Someone is not in his proper place.
Something is not quite right.
A forest felled and turned
is breaking into leaf.

Angel Hour

This morning I thought of the angels
I saw in a pre-dinner catnap
some years ago in Istria
and the tremendous crack
of thunder that same day
in a village where we lunched
on our way back to the coast.
I remember how they stood
in rank with their backs to me
on a road of golden clouds
that climbed into the sky
from our holiday bedroom.
Luminous, light as whispers,
I fancy they appeared
at the equidistant point
between lunch and dinner,
and wonder was that the point
of fasting in the old
church – vision's possibility,
the deeds of saints and martyrs,
the heights of Alvernia,
the desert and the voice
that cried in the wilderness?
The dry thunderclap
started me from my soup:
what I'd read about the war
came to mind though it never got
to the bistro we sat outside
on the borgo's single street.
I had ordered a second glass

of Pinot Grigio when *bang!*
a mortar shell behind me
blasted the afternoon.
But everything was OK,
the thunder merely a warning –
two glasses are enough –
and then the angels showed
in the stretch of abstinence
before the night's renewal
of appetite and glut.

The See-Through Poet

I can see clearly now
Through the see-through poet
But I'm disappointed by what I see
On the other side. I thought
That if I looked through him
I'd find something I could relate to
But no, there's nothing there
On the other side of the see-through poet
Only the blank wall of my own dismayed
And baffling existence.
But why am I looking
Beyond the see-through poet
Out through the back of his head
Into the back of beyond
Where I already am?
Should I not take his hand
And look into his eyes
Saying Savant, I do not comprehend,
Show me what it is I lack
To understand your enterprise
And how it can transport me
Halfway to the City of God.

Nothing Happened

I was pussyfooting past the Central Bank
as one does because it comes down upon one
passing by the Central Bank, the word
pussyfoot palpably enters the mind,
and in my earphones the talkers were talking
of what's being rolled out in the pipelines,
mincing their words and their metaphors. Then,
suddenly, nothing happened! It made me think
of Kavanagh frozen on a canal-bank seat
and the three-syllable word *homelessness*;
how relatively reticent are sheep
compared to dogs or cats. 'People should not
take bullshit from the laws of gravity',
I thought as I pussyfooted past the Central Bank.

The Wrong Kind of Dog

The sea tells me not in so many words
that all I'd care to say has been said before,
and that if anyone has said it well,
it's the old poets. So what am I doing here
in this creative bustle of the wind
and sky and sea, on a blustery shore
where everything is bobbing like a boat?
Houses, no longer in their stratified layers,
are joggling randomly around the cove,
a few hardy humans along the sand.
A seagull pauses in mid-air to watch.
And there's the yelping of unpleasant dogs
at odds on straining leashes with the wind
and also there's the yelping of the light,
harsh but not ear-splitting, as it strains
on the leash of the sun. Surely it is
a gale that's drumming up this mighty fuss,
though the wrong kind of dog is always found
on a strand. Old foamer in its oily coils,
the sea says all this has been said before,
drenching me in someone else's shoes.

Magritte

I am a man in a black bowler hat,
showing my back to the world.
If I turn, an apple blocks my face.

My first glimpse of art was in a churchyard,
so close is it to death.
I listened to the silence of that place.

Sometimes, laid out, she elevates behind me
as I walk the towpath.
Stiff-necked, I do not look around.

My art has no laws of gravity,
but a woman's chestnut hair falls to the ground
and bowler-hatted men are falling rain.

I have seen boulders floating in the sky,
and every day a cloud comes in my door.
Baguettes, instead of clouds, go drifting by.

In woods, between the horse's head and rider,
a vista slips, slim as the trunk of a tree:
what's visible hides what's also visible.

The sea is one with what is not the sea.

The Tree Outside my Window

There are many mansions in
the tree outside my window.

James Joyce is there, reciting
the sequel to *Finnegans Wake*
to oysters eating fillets of the rich
in its seafood restaurant,

and there's the repentant pope
nodding in total agreement
with the Marxist theologians
of its leafy constellations.

And the cringing olive-eyed
mongrel from down the lane
takes the evening paper
from his former master's mouth,

while the children of Peru
throw away their begging bowls
and screaming with delight
climb to the topmost branches.

O the fine ales the beautiful dead
drink in the tree outside my window!

Green is its darkness and its silver
in the breeze is starlight.

JOHN W. SEXTON

John W. Sexton was born in 1958, and lives in Kenmare in the West of Ireland. His sixth poetry collection, *Futures Pass*, was published by Salmon Poetry in 2018, and his seventh, *Visions at Templeglantine,* by Revival Press in 2020. His poem *The Green Owl* was awarded the Listowel Poetry Prize 2007 for best single poem, and in that same year he was awarded a Patrick and Katherine Kavanagh Fellowship in Poetry. His chapbook titled *Inverted Night* was published by SurVision Books in 2019.

The Face in your Mind

When the moon opens its three-quarters skull
I slip from its mask.

In moonlight and moonthought,
the moon's stain on roses,

I leave the taint of my light.

I am the after-image you'll get from a dream,
the memory that lingers from the memories
you never had but thought you did.

The Seeds of Gravity

An angel is divided into two by its wings

The right-handed wing is feathered cloud
skies without sunset
a slice of morning

The left-handed wing is a porcelain crescent
embossed with glazed vines

As the angel takes flight
the porcelain wing is shattered

Where its fragments fall
a new wild garden is sown

With its other wing the daytime sky is born in its
myriad hues

The Inverted Night

She plucks a lilac star from the sky.
It becomes an anti-star scented of emptiness:

the emptiness of the heavens beyond the heavens.

One by one the stars still left in the darkness
burst into petalled flowers. The sky blooms.

She observes that this is the reality of Physics.
She presents her observations in a paper to the Academy.

The Academy look in dismay at the findings she presents.
If the universe is a poem it will be infinitely unreachable.

A man writes a number onto a whiteboard.
The number is an invention. The Academy agree

that this is the true night. On the whiteboard a universe
begins to convince us it is there.

The Academy applauds the findings on their whiteboard.
Outside, the sky drops its fragrance on one who looks up.

The Snails

The snails prove in their individual kettles.
They think you into being.
You wake for the first time but are convinced it is a numerous morning.
The newly-minted world looks the way you imagined it always was.

The garden is a square of perfect grass.
You dig it up into a square of perfect earth.
You set a perfect aspirational garden.
You sleep your first night but are convinced there were others.

You wake for the second time but think it is a numerous morning.
The glass in all of the windows is studded with snails.
You look in disgust at their oily bodies.
They threaten to become punctuations to the perfection of your hopes.

The snails are a pestilence upon your creation.
You pick them off the windows and collect them in a bucket.
You pull them from the newly-set cabbages you invented.
You created this world and will not let it be marred.

You sleep your second night.
You wake for the third time but are convinced it is a numerous
morning.
On the way to somewhere there is silver writing all over the pavement.
It is a gospel you imagine always was.

The Changing Room

In the changing room she tried on a yellow dress
and looked at herself in the long mirror.

But the yellow dress was a mask, not a dress,
so all she could see was a stranger in a blue coat.

She removed the yellow dress and tried on a blue coat.
But the blue coat was a mask, so she saw nothing

in the long mirror but the onrush of pines in her descent
from the blistered moonlit sky.

She took off the blue coat and tried on a snowy owl.
The snowy owl was a tight fit but she persevered

and squeezed herself all the way into it.
But the snowy owl was a mask, so all she could see

was herself in a yellow dress, weary from endless pretence.

Incidents of the Night

Moonlight licked grass, the still trees, the southern
windows all at once. In your sleep you turned
to the wall, breathed at its discourse of damp.
A dead moon in the corner, (shadeless lamp),
dreamt that it could dream: memories of light
in its fused mind. Outside, badgers moved night
with their sheer wills. In your sleep you turned south.
Snoring, you exhaled a cord from your mouth.
The cord shrivelled on contact with the air,
became a dribble on the pillow. Hair
gathered itself in the plughole, braided
itself; then forgot where it was headed.
From the pond a gathered-man of frogspawn,
with your name on his tongue, trod through the lawn.

How a Leech House Eats a House

The builders moved in on the twenty-third,
arrived with no notice of their coming.
In the long months they were seen but not heard,
for dead hammering is no hammering.
Rooms appeared inside our own; bright, spectral
as frogspawn jelly; eyeless, yes, but cold.
Superimposed, rooms shone electrical
when the lights were off; our windows blazed bold
lozenges through night. New tenants settled
into us, our bones lit from within. Time
lost its meaning, space became unsettled
until we were simply shadows, a mime
cast by the new dwellers. Our tenancy
done, we entered eternal vacancy.

The Isn't Bus

An eye has risen over the city
and weeps its green lye. The city is as thin
as light; it blinks in and out; here now, gone now.
The street is and isn't. I take the isn't bus.
At the lights the bus is. On entering the bus station
the bus isn't. We disembark into a pale flame.
Moths as large as coats expire as smoke
in the air around us. A woman begins combing
sound from her hair. The sound flocks
in the brightness above us, a liquid ball of dark;
it coagulates over the city. One by one
single chimes fall from the sky. The concrete forecourt
of the bus station is littered with starlings,
now fluttering soundlessly at our feet.
A man removes faces from his briefcase
and distributes them to everyone nearby.
The face he has given me is disconsolate. I pull it over
my head and it slips into place. Another bus
enters the station and we embark. We ask
to be taken nowhere and the driver kills the
engine. In the stillness of the darkened bus
we wait without any expectation whatsoever.

Lucifer's Bulb in His Head

Brains to burn, his mind was a lump of lard.
When he thought, he thought his thoughts unheard;
strains of binary pathways, strings of code.
Hens pecked at the thinking he'd left scattered.
Archetypes were scratched in the mud by claws
of angels fallen to the mucky yard;
though not the Angels of God – but simply
parasites moving through Heaven. Nine, nine,

nine, nine: sigils stark with emergency.
Listen, listen. Hold vigils for the voice
of reason. Not the voice of yourself, not
thoughts birthing grey mould like his thoughts birthed.
Brains to burn, his mind was a lump of lard;
when he thought, his thoughts were deathly loud.

The Cyclopean Train Approaching Kulosaari

The man with the umbrella made from bats' wings
is shaking the rain into your face. Each raindrop
is the memory of a missed train. In each train
is a woman with freckles like the spots on a lynx.
Then her face is a lynx's face; there's a pleading
songbird between her teeth. The umbrella
of bats' wings takes to the air, makes a path
through the clouds of flies that have been deputised
as the sun. Suddenly the sun is shattered
into fragments of black glass. You pick a piece
from the ground and your finger bleeds straight away.
It bleeds uncontrollably and you have no choice
but to put your finger into your mouth. Then a train as red
as your bloody finger enters the platform. It is the train
that you have missed all your life. The doors open
with a hiss. The sky above is a deep green. Now is now.

More poetry published by SurVision Books

Noelle Kocot. *Humanity*
(New Poetics: USA)
ISBN 978-1-9995903-0-7

Ciaran O'Driscoll. *The Speaking Trees*
(New Poetics: Ireland)
ISBN 978-1-9995903-1-4

Helen Ivory. *Maps of the Abandoned City*
(New Poetics: England)
ISBN 978-1-912963-04-1

Elin O'Hara Slavick. *Cameramouth*
(New Poetics: USA)
ISBN 978-1-9995903-4-5

John W. Sexton. *Inverted Night*
(New Poetics: Ireland)
ISBN 978-1-912963-05-8

Afric McGlinchey. *Invisible Insane*
(New Poetics: Ireland)
ISBN 978-1-9995903-3-8

Anatoly Kudryavitsky. *Stowaway*
(New Poetics: Ireland)
ISBN 978-1-9995903-2-1

Tim Murphy. *The Cacti Do Not Move*
(New Poetics: Ireland)
ISBN 978-1-912963-07-2

Tony Kitt. *The Magic Phlute*
(New Poetics: Ireland)
ISBN 978-1-912963-08-9

Clayre Benzadón. *Liminal Zenith*
(New Poetics: USA)
ISBN 978-1-912963-11-9

Thomas Townsley. *Tangent of Ardency*
(New Poetics: USA)
ISBN 978-1-912963-15-7

Matthew Geden. *Fruit*
(New Poetics: Ireland)
ISBN 978-1-912963-16-4

George Kalamaras. *That Moment of Wept*
ISBN 978-1-9995903-7-6

Anton Yakovlev. *Chronos Dines Alone*
(Winner of James Tate Poetry Prize 2018)
ISBN 978-1-912963-01-0

Bob Lucky. *Conversation Starters in a Language No One Speaks*
(Winner of James Tate Poetry Prize 2018)
ISBN 978-1-912963-00-3

Christopher Prewitt. *Paradise Hammer*
(Winner of James Tate Poetry Prize 2018)
ISBN 978-1-9995903-9-0

Mikko Harvey & Jake Bauer. *Idaho Falls*
(Winner of James Tate Poetry Prize 2018)
ISBN 978-1-912963-02-7

Tony Bailie. *Mountain Under Heaven*
(Winner of James Tate Poetry Prize 2019)
ISBN 978-1-912963-09-6

Nicholas Alexander Hayes. *Amorphous Organics*
(Winner of James Tate Poetry Prize 2019)
ISBN 978-1-912963-10-2

John Bradley. *Spontaneous Mummification*
(Winner of James Tate Poetry Prize 2019)
ISBN 978-1-912963-13-3

John Thomas Allen. *Rolling in the Third Eye*
(Winner of James Tate Poetry Prize 2019)
ISBN 978-1-912963-15-7

Gary Glauber. *The Covalence of Equanimity*
(Winner of James Tate Poetry Prize 2019)
ISBN 978-1-912963-12-6

Maria Grazia Calandrone. *Fossils*
Translated from Italian
(New Poetics: Italy)
ISBN 978-1-9995903-6-9

Sergey Biryukov. *Transformations*
Translated from Russian
(New Poetics: Russia)
ISBN 978-1-9995903-5-2

Alexander Korotko. *Irrazionalismo*
Translated from Russian
(New Poetics: Ukraine)
ISBN 978-1-912963-06-5

Anton G. Leitner. *Selected Poems 1981–2015*
Translated from German
ISBN 978-1-9995903-8-3

**message-door: An Anthology of Contemporary Surrealist
Poetry from Russia** (bilingual)
Edited and translated from Russian by Anatoly Kudryavitsky
ISBN 978-1-912963-17-1

All our books are available to order via
http://survisionmagazine.com/books.htm